YOUR PERSONAL LEADERSHIP COACH

THE FIRST STEP OF YOUR JOURNEY

BY

CHRISTOPHER D. WATERS

I

Table of Contents

Introduction

I started my journey to become a leadership coach in July 2001 when I took command of my first platoon in the Marine Corps. As a twenty-three year old second lieutenant, I was placed responsible and accountable for over forty young men and women. I had heard the word "leadership" many times through my years of playing football and baseball, but had never fully grasped its weight until that day. My Marines had to be willing to follow me into combat, into situations that could mean their lives. I realized their families and loved ones had to place their trust in my leadership to make sure their Marine came home to them. From that day on, I devoted myself to grow as a leader, and to ensure that I was worthy enough to lead Marines. Not only was it my responsibility to effectively lead my Marines, it was my responsibility to develop them as leaders as well.

This book is intended to help you discover coaching for yourself without the pressure of the sales process. Many people misperceive coaching to be an expert telling them how they should lead or improve as a leader. That is not leadership coaching. I will introduce to you a taste of what coaching is and reveal how leadership coaching can help you discover the leader within yourself. I will introduce and lay out how coaching is different from teaching and mentoring. Moreover, you will benefit from an introduction to coaching without making a commitment that you are unsure you want to make. I will mention that this book is not a replacement for what the coaching process has to offer. A one on one coaching relationship between a coach and client cannot be duplicated in a book. The true value of coaching is found in the questions that are triggered by a client's answers. It is the curiosity to drive deeper, on the part of the coach, which gives greater value to the coaching process.

I believe that coaching can transform how people in positions of authority lead and think about leadership. My vision is to create a culture that is populated by leaders rather than followers. Moral leaders who care for their people enough to serve and develop them as leaders. I invite you to take an important step in your leadership journey, and more importantly, discover that the answers you seek reside within you.

What Is Leadership Coaching?

"Teachers share their knowledge. Mentors share their experiences, while coaches share in your journey." – Chris Waters

It is easy to learn from leadership experts how they lead. It's easy to note the principles they believe and practice, and work to apply what we have learned from those experts. In reality, though we miss out on a lot of what is taught, because our reality is not the same as the expert's reality. As a society, there is one person we have missed out on learning from, and that is ourselves. We are a wealth of untapped knowledge and potential. Modern technologies, like our cell phones and televisions, have muffled our minds and our inner voice. We spend very little time in complete silence, allowing our minds to drift and explore what we already know, but have yet to discover. The universe we seek to chart is not out of reach. It's right here inside us all, if we take the time to embark on the journey.

Coaching is a relationship where a coach and a client embark on a journey together through the mind, heart, and soul of the client. The relationship is entirely focused on the benefit of the client, but requires one hundred percent commitment to the process from both the coach and the client. A good coach has an insatiable curiosity about his client, which is critical to asking deep, thought provoking questions. They are a person of character who is completely invested in his client's success. The entire relationship is designed to stimulate thought, raise awareness, increase responsibility, create an environment of accountability, and empower a client to discover the answers to the questions she has for herself. The irony of a successful coach is they spend more time listening than speaking. If the right questions are asked, the client spends most of the time doing the talking. The results can completely alter a person's way of thinking, therefore their way of living. It is a process that takes time. It is not a sprint.

Our actions and behaviors are what contribute to our success, and it's our beliefs that dictate our actions and behaviors. Teaching can tell you what you should believe. A mentor may even demonstrate his beliefs, actions and behaviors, but when you work with a coach, you discover why you act and behave the way you do; therefore, you become consciously aware of that to which you were once blind. Knowing what to change and how is good information, but not knowing your own truth regarding why this change must happen for you will not make change sustainable. Coaching helps people discover that the changes they seek can be attained through an awareness that challenges and even changes what they believe about the world. When beliefs change, then so do actions and behaviors. You don't have to work so hard at the actions and behaviors when what you believe drives you. Over time, you adopt a new subconscious. What once required deliberate attention to act upon now becomes something you do without thinking, until you decide to grow some more. This is the cycle of self-development.

You might be thinking: "Oh, you know the answers, so you ask questions that guide me to the right answers." No, that is not coaching either. A good coach does not have an agenda and does not guide her client to an answer that she believes her client should arrive at. The agenda is actually set by the client prior to each session. It is irresponsible for a coach to guide a client to an answer that they believe is correct for the client. My reality that got me to where I am as a man and leader is not the same reality for you. That is why a responsible coach does not guide his client. The most valuable lessons in exploration are the lessons learned from taking wrong turns. Unless a client is heading down a path to catastrophe and the coach can prevent it, the coach is to allow the process to run its course. This is where real learning, true discovery, and actual transformation occur. The answers you discover through the coaching process are not notes you have to jot down and reference later. Those answers are now innate within you through an awakened self-awareness. It is just like learning how to ride a bike. Anyone who knows how has fallen countless times before mastering it. Now, even if it has been years since you last rode, you know you can hop on and go. We did not sit in a class and take notes on how to ride a bike, we experienced it. This is why I love coaching people and helping them become more effective leaders. It is a joy to witness the awakening in a person. And it's quite a gift to realize that each of us is already walking around with the answers we seek.

Leadership is critical to security and prosperity in our society. From war, to politics, to business, leadership is the root cause of success or failure. There are countless programs out there that teach leadership skills. And there is nothing wrong with learning key leadership principles, but my opinion is that they do not go far enough. There is a difference between practicing leadership and living as a leader. Leadership comes from our morals, values, and beliefs. Our character defines the leader we are, more so than any skills we learn in a class environment. Leadership coaching drives a client deep within himself to find the unique leader that resides within. Instead of trying to remember something that was taught to you, you draw on what is innate and is part of you. Principles taught are quickly forgotten, but principles discovered from within through coaching are never forgotten.

Now that I have briefly introduced what coaching is, what follows are some coaching questions designed to stimulate your thinking and give you a glimpse of what coaching can do for you. I will remind you that one of the great benefits of coaching comes from follow-up questions to answers you give. A good coach immerses himself into each session with his client. With every shared answer, thought, and shift in body language, a good coach has a curiosity to drive deeper and deeper into his client's subconscious. You will not have that benefit in reading this book, because I obviously don't know what your answers will be. Use this book to begin your journey and decide how leadership coaching could benefit you. There are lines for you to write your answers. Treat this book like a work book. It is a simple and short format. You don't have to power read your way through it. Don't hesitate to use a note pad to capture your answers and allow everything in you to flow on to the paper. I ask that you take your time and think carefully about each question asked, as well as the answer. I have often had clients talk through their thoughts for nearly an hour after asking them a simple question, and that is a good thing! It is my hope and intention to ask the right questions that stimulate deep thought about your own personal leadership. That is where your own infinite wisdom can be found. I wish you good fortune on your journey.

Why Are You Here?

What compelled you to pick up this book?

This is a simple, yet often overlooked, question because many people are too busy to allow themselves the time required to give this question deep thought. We accept what others and the media tell us to think instead of allowing our own thoughts to come to light. I find that waking up earlier than everyone in the house and sitting in complete silence and darkness allows me to think. Short side note: I once was sitting thinking when the power went out. It was amazing how much noise was eliminated when that happened. We have become so numb to the humming of a fridge or furnace that we are not even aware of some sounds until they are actually eliminated. Make an effort to find complete silence. Give yourself the opportunity to hear your own wisdom.

Take the time now to ask yourself and answer these questions:

Why did you pick up this book?

Curiosity? Personal Development? Professional Development? Bored on a plane? Hey, I've done it more times than I can remember. What do you hope to find? Or learn?

_____

_____

_____

_____

_____

_____

_____

_____

_____

What do you desire to change about yourself, or about your life, or both?

Take time to really dial in on what it is you want to change or improve. Allow yourself to daydream about what your life looks like with those changes made.

_____

_____

_____

_____

_____

_____

_____

_____

_____

Ask yourself: "What am I willing to do or sacrifice for those changes to become reality?"

_____

_____

_____

_____

_____

_____

_____

_____

_____

_____

**What has happened in your life to make you desire
change? Or, what is driving your curiosity for
change? Or, what hasn't happened?**

Sometimes, we either experience events in our lives that is

a pivot point to make us want to change, or we have been

stagnant for far too long, and we need to shake things up

to stimulate growth and change in our lives.

_____

_____

_____

_____

_____

_____

_____

_____

_____

_____

What do you hope to learn about yourself through this process?

What is your hidden talent or hidden strengths that you have not fully realized and acted on? Why?

_____

_____

_____

_____

_____

_____

_____

_____

_____

What about you and your life makes you believe that?

_____

_____

_____

_____

_____

_____

What has prevented you from exploring that until now?

_____

_____

_____

_____

_____

_____

Do you fear what you may learn about yourself? If so why?

Sometimes we may not like what we find about ourselves. There are risks to taking journeys within. I remember how I felt when I left for the Marines. I was about to find out if I had what it takes to earn the title United States Marine. There was only one way to find out, and that was to jump right in. I know people who try to observe challenges from the outside, looking in, and attempt to assess if they are capable of conquering that challenge. They think they can measure who they are and what they are made of from a safe place. Unfortunately, it does not work that way.

_____

_____

_____

_____

_____

_____

_____

_____

_____

_____

**What are the consequences for learning something
that you don't like about yourself?**

Many of us avoid knowing things we don't like about

ourselves. Many know the truth but attempt to conceal or

deny it. What can acknowledge that truth do to you?

What kind of person can use that knowledge to her

advantage? Are you that kind of person?

_____

_____

_____

_____

_____

_____

_____

What can you do about those consequences?

_____

_____

_____

_____

_____

_____

_____

_____

_____

If you have the will to make the changes necessary, what
are those changes? What is preventing you from starting
now?

_____

_____

_____

_____

_____

_____

_____

_____

_____

_____

What is the limit to your potential?

Our environment is shaped by what we believe to be true.
Those who maximize their potential believe there is no
limit to their potential. Feel that discomfort? We very well
may be challenging one of your beliefs right now. That's a
good thing. That is a boundary that you must challenge
and break through. If you retreat from that boundary,
you will remain bound!

_____

_____

_____

_____

_____

_____

_____

_____

_____

_____

What could you achieve if you knew that there was no
limit to your potential?

_____

_____

_____

_____

_____

_____

_____

_____

_____

_____

What reason is there for placing a limit on your potential?

_____

_____

_____

_____

_____

What beliefs are you willing to sail off the edge of the world for?

Think about it this way: Christopher Columbus lived in a world that was flat. He was willing to risk sailing off the edge of the world to prove it was round, a belief that had never been proven before.

_____

_____

_____

_____

_____

_____

_____

_____

_____

What are the consequences if you fail? Are you
capable of recovering from them? How do you know?
I like to help people put failure into perspective. Watch a
child who is learning to walk. If you place a toy they want
across a room, they will stop at nothing to get to it. They
will fall a dozen times before reaching their goal. Can you
recall how many times you fell? You most likely can't. Do
you consider yourself a failure since you fell so many
times? You most likely don't. Why? Because you found
success after trying and trying until you mastered it.

_____

_____

_____

_____

_____

_____

_____

_____

_____

_____

Why were you willing to fall so many times?

_____

_____

_____

_____

Why were you not afraid after falling the first time?

_____

_____

_____

_____

_____

_____

What were the consequences?

_____

_____

_____

_____

_____

_____

_____

What are the consequences to falling today?

_____

_____

_____

_____

_____

_____

If the consequence is a price too high to pay, what is the alternative?

_____

_____

_____

_____

_____

_____

What aspects of your personal and/or professional life are unfulfilled? Do you know?

Have you ever taken the time to actually articulate what is holding you back? Have you taken the time to run through how you feel about your work performance, finances, leadership effectiveness, professional relationships, personal relationships? And, how all those are related and may affect one another? What is the common theme that holds you back?

_____

_____

_____

_____

_____

_____

_____

_____

_____

_____

What results are you working to achieve?

What are you working toward today? Are those efforts in

line with your goals? Why?

_____

_____

_____

_____

_____

_____

_____

_____

What goal or result would you like to achieve? Why?

_____

_____

_____

_____

_____

_____

_____

How are you maximizing your efforts to achieve that goal

or goals?

_____

_____

_____

_____

_____

_____

_____

Do you have a plan to achieve it? If so, what is it? If not, why not?

_____

_____

_____

_____

_____

_____

_____

_____

_____

Where do you see yourself a year from now?

I ask my clients to commit to a minimum of six months, with a preferred commitment of a year, because leadership coaching is not a sprint or a quick fix. It takes time. When I start off with a client, one of my first questions is this: What will your life look like in a year? Where do you plan to be professionally and personally? Can you

describe it in detail? If so, do so.

_____

_____

_____

_____

_____

_____

_____

_____

_____

_____

_____

_____

How will these changes affect how you live every day?

Can you describe what every day will be like, once you achieve the changes you desire? Are you able to envision the details from the time you wake up, the coffee you drink, and times you start and stop working, the time you spend with your loved ones, even when you take the dog for a walk, etc...? Be specific about what better looks like. You have to see it in your mind before you create it in reality.

_____

_____

_____

_____

_____

_____

_____

_____

_____

_____

_____

What level of commitment do you have to making the necessary changes required to get there?

On a scale of 1 to 10, rate your level of commitment, then describe what that commitment requires in actions. Example 10 is the level of commitment that you will get out of bed tomorrow morning. It's that certain. Anything lower than 9 is not a full commitment.

_____

_____

_____

_____

_____

_____

_____

_____

_____

_____

_____

_____

Reminder: Take it slow. You can take as long as you want thinking about the answers. There is no deadline. Reflect on the answers you have written. If you have not written any, take the time to do so. Allow yourself to use your God-given gift of thought. The greatest creations our world has ever experienced were first dreams and ideas.

What is Your Purpose?

Knowing your purpose affords you the luxury to focus your actions on tasks that help you live your purpose. Without a purpose, you live life at random, or worse, your daily tasks are to fulfill someone else's purpose.

A simple question to ask can be very tough to answer. What is your purpose? There are very few people who know early on in their lives what their purpose is. My sister is one such person. She is an elementary school teacher who has known since she was a little girl that she wanted to be a teacher. She would come home from school, place her dolls in front of a chalk board, and do her homework while pretending to teach them. If you grew up like her, knowing your purpose, this is a piece of cake. If you are like the majority of people, however, you graduated college or high school, got a job, and ended up stuck in a profession that you grew to learn, but had never intended to pursue. For some reason, discovering our purpose is not part of our formal education. We are groomed to learn skills that help us find employment. It is left up to the individual to step outside the status quo to find her purpose, and walk a path that allows them to live it.

When we align our purpose with our morals and values, all three are reflected in our decisions and actions. When we are clear on what our purpose is, everything we do has a laser focus on living that purpose. Knowing our purpose makes us influential. People will want to align what they believe with you. You will attract, and be attracted to, those who share what you believe. Even if you are currently working a monotonous job with aspirations of leaving that job one day, the most important step you can take towards leaving is identifying, articulating, and living your purpose. The path you are looking for will then be laid before you.

What were the times you were the happiest?

Think all the way back to your childhood and trace your steps to the present. You may not remember moments, but do you remember time periods of happiness?

_____

_____

_____

_____

_____

_____

_____

What role did others have in your happiness?

_____

_____

_____

_____

_____

_____

Why were you happiest then?

_____

_____

_____

_____

_____

_____

What did you do that made you so happy?

_____

_____

_____

_____

_____

_____

_____

What about what you were doing made you happy?

_____

_____

_____

_____

_____

_____

_____

What were the times when you felt the most

significant or the most fulfilled?

When did you feel that you had the greatest impact on

others or the world? Was there a time when you felt you

were making a difference? Was there a time when you

were able to put in long hours and walk away from a day

with the feeling of accomplishment?

_____

_____

_____

_____

_____

_____

_____

_____

_____

_____

What about what you were doing that stimulated those

feelings?

_____

_____

_____

_____

_____

_____

_____

What were you going to be when you grew up?

Reflect on your childhood dreams. Why were we such dreamers as children and less so today? What great things were you going to accomplish when you grew up?

_____

_____

_____

_____

_____

_____

_____

_____

_____

How could you still make them happen?

_____

_____

_____

_____

_____

_____

_____

_____

_____

_____

If not exactly living your dream, what other creative ways
could you make that dream come true?

_____

_____

_____

_____

_____

What is holding you back?

_____

_____

_____

_____

_____

_____

_____

Are those obstacles real or perceived? Why?

_____

_____

_____

_____

_____

What can you do to overcome them?

_____

_____

_____

_____

_____

_____

_____

What happened that caused you to surrender that dream? When?

Those who don't live their dream, encountered that moment that their dream died. You may actually remember the exact moment it happened. Why did you surrender? Was it physical ability? Was it discouraging words from friends or family?

_____

_____

_____

_____

_____

_____

_____

_____

_____

Was it ever proven that you could not achieve that dream?
What is the proof?

_____

_____

_____

_____

_____

_____

_____

If there was never proof, why not pursue it now?

_____

_____

_____

_____

_____

_____

If you could rewind the clock, could you change that moment your dream died? If so, what would you change? Is that change impossible to make today? Is it really too late? Why?

_____

_____

_____

_____

_____

_____

_____

What are the consequences if you rekindle that dream and fail at trying today?

_____

_____

_____

_____

_____

_____

_____

If you faltered, what actions could you take to recover?

_____

_____

_____

_____

_____

_____

Is there any way to rekindle that fire? If not, are there alternate paths?

My childhood dream was to play for the Pittsburgh Steelers. I love football, but after playing seventeen seasons, and having played in both high school and college, I recognizing that my talents did not reside in football. I realized that was beyond reality for me, but through that dream fading, I pursued my secondary dream to become a United States Marine. I discovered a passion I always had, but never fully recognized, and that is a service to something higher. A service to what makes America great, and to my fellow man. Eventually it made way to what my purpose is today, which is to improve, secure, and protect the future of America. I live my purpose by helping others maximize their leadership potential.

Through your life's journey, what has become your calling? Having a purpose is not so much about the pursuit of it, but more so about the feeling pursuing that purpose gives us. What gives you that feeling of significance?

_____

_____

_____

_____

_____

_____

_____

_____

_____

What would it take for you to begin pursuing that dream?

Most people desire perfect circumstances to trigger their pursuit of their dreams. A lot of times it's a financial state that people site in order to begin. There may be other reasons as well.

_____

_____

_____

_____

_____

_____

_____

_____

What sacrifices would you have to make to start today?

_____

_____

_____

_____

_____

_____

_____

What sacrifices are you willing to make?

_____

_____

_____

_____

_____

And which are you unwilling to make?

_____

_____

_____

_____

_____

_____

_____

Is it a waste of your time to write down a dream map or
plan?   Sometimes thinking through and mentally
navigating the plan for your dreams allow you the
opportunity to realize that it is not as daunting as
originally perceived. Most often it only requires
commitment and discipline.   Is there anything preventing
you from beginning right this second? If so, what is it? Is
it real or perceived?

_____

_____

_____

_____

_____

_____

_____

What is the worst that would happen if you started

anyway, regardless of the obstacles?

_____

_____

_____

_____

_____

_____

_____

After reflecting on your life's path, your childhood dreams

and passions, ask yourself:

What are you good at?

We often look right past what our hobby is and what we

have mastered through that hobby because we think we

can't make money at it, or we think there are a lot of

people already doing it and have perfected it. Don't sell

yourself short. Often, the difference between great and

average is courage and action. Throughout your life, what have you always been good at?

_____

_____

_____

_____

_____

_____

_____

In what areas of your life have things come naturally? What subjects have you always had clarity in understanding that others have struggled?

_____

_____

_____

_____

_____

_____

_____

If you don't know what you are good at, are you willing to find out? How could you find out?

_____

_____

_____

_____

_____

What is your perspective on failure? How do you handle it? Do you fear it? Or embrace it?

Failure is only failure if you choose not to get up.

I often tell people that the formula to success is "Passion + Purpose = The Power to Persevere." When you have passion and purpose in clear sight, you are willing to fail over and over again, because you don't view it as failure. You view it as learning in pursuit of whatever your passion or purpose is. Some of the greatest inventors and explorers are known for their great achievements. We must dig into their journeys to realize they failed many times over before they found their fame and success. What made them willing to fail so many times was not that they had money or the right conditions or time, but rather, it was all they thought about and dreamed about. Failure was not failure to them. It was a challenge. From the Wright Brothers to Thomas Edison, the formula rings true. "Passion + Purpose = The Power to Persevere." The Wright Brothers crashed many times before they took flight. Thomas Edison blew up his lab countless times before perfecting the light bulb.

What are you willing to fail at one thousand times or more and keep pursuing? What are you so passionate about that you are willing to fail, learn, fail again, learn more, and repeat that cycle over and over until you achieve your vision?

_____

_____

_____

_____

_____

_____

_____

_____

_____

_____

What expertise do you have that people are always asking you to share?

Whether at work or at home, what do people come to you for the most? Do your friends and family seek your advice and expertise for any specific subject matter? Why?

_____

_____

_____

_____

_____

_____

_____

_____

_____

_____

_____

What is it you have to offer, that others don't, when people

seek you out?

_____

_____

_____

_____

_____

_____

What is unique about you that make them feel

comfortable to ask you?

_____

_____

_____

_____

_____

_____

Why do you feel confident being their source of advice?

_____

_____

_____

_____

_____

What questions do you jump at answering?

What subjects excite you when you hear people talking?
Have you ever overheard people discussing a specific
subject that you have interest in and you have an
uncontrollable urge to weigh in? What are those subjects?
What about them interests you so much?

_____

_____

_____

_____

_____

_____

_____

_____

_____

_____

_____

_____

_____

_____

_____

What common themes exist from your answers?

Refer to the answers to the questions above. What themes
do you see in your answers? What consistencies do you
see?

_____

_____

_____

_____

_____

_____

_____

_____

_____

_____

What common feelings are generated by those themes?

_____

_____

_____

_____

_____

_____

_____

Exercises1: Write out what your dream life of living your purpose would look like.

Write below or on sheet of paper or in a journal, write out exactly what your dream life would look like. This is where self-limiting thoughts are going to creep in and attempt to knock you back into your comfort zone. You must throw out all attempts to limit yourself. Use your answers to the above questions to help you form this new vision. Do not allow self-doubt around what your mind tells you is realistic to limit you. For example, if you desire your annual income to become your monthly income, write that down. Walk yourself through what a day and a week would look like living your purpose and dream. Write down every detail from waking up, the house you are in as you get ready for your day, the car you drive to work, to going to bed. Revisit this exercise a few days from now, and don't read your previous response. The reason is so you can compare what you wrote the first time to what you wrote the second time.

_____

_____

_____

_____

_____

_____

_____

_____

_____

After multiple writings, take the two or three responses and read them. Write down the most obvious and consistent themes. What feelings are prevalent that you desire to have for yourself? What daily and weekly routines ring throughout what you have written in every response? How do those commonalities line up with your dreams?

_____

_____

_____

_____

_____

_____

_____

_____

_____

_____

_____

Exercise 2: Write your purpose statement

Take all that information and put it into a purpose statement.

For example, here is my purpose:

To improve, secure, and protect the future of the United States of America, so that our children and our children's children live in freedom and prosperity.

Write your purpose statement multiple times, as you did when you wrote your desired daily and weekly life. Make sure that what you end up with gives you a visceral feeling, something you can't explain. You just know that how that statement makes you feel is right. You feel completed by that statement, you feel significant, and you feel confident in saying it to anyone.

_____

_____

_____

_____

_____

_____

_____

_____

Live your purpose every day

Start today. There is no time like the present. Begin living your purpose in every small and large way possible. I have no doubt you lead a busy life. Don't worry about the money. That will work itself out. Live your purpose where ever you are. If you want to help people, start with family, friends, or work colleagues. Seek out educational opportunities such as books, certifications, training, and seminars. Make time for your purpose.

If you don't have enough time in your day, make it. Get up earlier, or go to bed later. Don't allow the excuse of time stop you. I have no doubt you have something in your day that you can eliminate to make time for your purpose, because here is a very true statement: When you are laying on your death-bed, you will not measure your success by the money in your bank account as much as by the impact you had on the world. That impact is most likely found in the self-worth, fulfillment, and purpose you have for yourself. Would you regret not finding that extra time? If the answer is yes, here is your chance to negate that regret.

Would You Follow You?

"The toughest person to lead is always yourself." – John C.
Maxwell

Temecula, CA of January 15th, 2003, I was a twenty-five year old 1st Lieutenant. In fewer than 30 days my unit would be leaving for Kuwait in the staging of what would become Operation Iraqi Freedom. That morning, just like every morning, I stood looking in the mirror in my camouflage uniform. That morning, just like every morning, I asked myself: *"Would I follow me into combat?"* I would imagine myself standing in formation, as one of my Marines, staring back at me. Was I upright? Was I true? Was I trust worthy? Would I trust my judgement? In the midst of chaos and uncertainty, would I find calm and courage in me? Would my family find comfort in knowing I was leading me? Would I sacrifice my life for me? I imagined that these were the questions my Marines asked of me. I owed them the respect of asking the same of myself. I operated with the thought that if I was to ask my Marines to follow me, I should be willing to follow myself. If I wasn't, then I was not worthy enough to be their leader.

That time in my life was years before I knew what leadership coaching was. No one taught me to ask those questions of myself. I believe it was God's guidance. I had an overwhelming compulsion to make sure that if I was to ask my Marines to follow me, I must be willing to do the same. There could be no excuse. The toughest part of asking myself this question was that I knew all my strengths and weaknesses. What was equally as tough was having the discipline to not permit myself to look past the slightest hesitations when I questioned myself. We may think slight chinks in our armor are insignificant, but we must accept the possibility that those we lead don't see it that way.

As leaders, it's almost instinctual to deny we have leadership flaws. Some leaders feel that acknowledging their shortcomings is an indictment of their character. Far too often, we allow our intentions to cloud our ability to observe how we truly make the people we lead feel. It's a common human flaw to be blind to the fact that we measure those who lead us by how they make us feel, and when we are leaders, it's natural to be frustrated when people don't understand our intentions. This is where leaders discover the ability to lead themselves. When leaders can step outside themselves, look back at themselves, and accept that their communications are not measured by their intentions, but rather, by how they make people feel, that is when growth as a leader takes off.

Who was the best leader you ever had?

Think back to a time when you had a leader for whom you loved work. What about that leader made you want to follow him? How did he make you feel? You may not remember everything he said as much as how you felt around him.

_____

_____

_____

_____

_____

_____

_____

_____

_____

_____

What characteristics did they possess that attracted you

to their leadership?

_____

_____

_____

_____

_____

_____

_____

Who was the worst leader you ever had?

This leader is normally the easiest to remember, even

though we may try hard to forget them. Ironically, this is

a leader from whom we can learn the most. How did this

leader make you feel? What did he do to make you feel

that way?

_____

_____

_____

_____

_____

_____

_____

_____

_____

_____

_____

What characteristics repelled you? Probably, as you are

picturing him in your head, how he made you feel has

crept back inside you. What is that feeling you are

feeling? Capture it.

_____

_____

_____

_____

_____

_____

_____

_____

How did he get to his position of leadership? What was he responsible for?

_____

_____

_____

_____

_____

_____

_____

What about him, if he would have changed, would have made him a better leader?

_____

_____

_____

_____

_____

_____

_____

If you had to follow you, what traits would you find strong and attractive in your leadership?

Often, it's the positives about us that are the toughest to describe. What characteristics about you would you feel inspired to follow? What of your strengths would inspire you or empower you, if you had to follow you every day?

_____

_____

_____

_____

_____

_____

_____

_____

_____

_____

_____

_____

Why are those traits your strongest?

_____

_____

_____

_____

_____

_____

_____

Why do you believe they are your strongest? What

indications have you witnessed that prove those traits are

your strongest?

_____

_____

_____

_____

_____

_____

_____

_____

_____

_____

What results have they produced? Are those traits

enough to make you excited to want to follow you every

day?

_____

_____

_____

_____

_____

_____

_____

_____

_____

_____

_____

What are the negative traits about you that would make you not want to follow yourself?

This can be a difficult line of thought at first. Most people in leadership positions have an unconscious belief that any weakness in their leadership is a character flaw. It's quite the opposite. The question is not whether or not we have them. We all do, and that's a fact. The question is how honest we are with ourselves about them, and what actions do we take to minimize them or eliminate them?

Take a moment. Look at yourself objectively. What traits do you have that would make you not want to follow you? Or, not enjoy following you? The key here is to not breeze past something that you just made you hesitate. Go back to that hesitation and dive deeper. What was it? It could be how you greet people, or how you assign tasks, or maybe you hesitated on how you don't show enough appreciation, or that you haven't taken the time to get to know your people well. Don't discard these thoughts and assume they are insignificant. We are tightening every screw, not just the obvious ones. Believe it or not, that may be a trait or weakness that is impacting the most people you lead. You may even have a trait that people have criticized you about in the past and you deny. Remember, perception is reality.

_____

_____

_____

_____

_____

_____

_____

_____

_____

_____

_____

_____

_____

Why do people perceive that of you? Consider that that criticism is correct for a moment. How would your level of influence change if you took action to improve on that criticism?

_____

_____

_____

_____

_____

_____

_____

_____

_____

_____

If that criticism is true, would you want to follow yourself with that flawed trait? Why?

_____

_____

_____

_____

_____

_____

_____

How would following you with those traits impact your

productivity and motivation?

_____

_____

_____

_____

_____

_____

_____

_____

_____

How would you feel about your leader if you knew she was taking action in order to improve as a leader?

_____

_____

_____

_____

_____

_____

_____

_____

_____

_____

What are your values?

What do you value in life? Are these values reflected in how you lead? How?

_____

_____

_____

_____

_____

_____

_____

_____

Can you describe how you demonstrate your values?

What values do your daily decisions and actions

communicate to your people?

_____

_____

_____

_____

_____

_____

_____

_____

If you value work life balance, are you sending your people emails over the weekend? Whatever your values are, are you doing anything that contradicts those values in the slightest? This is a foundational cause of people not trusting their leaders. They hear one thing, but see something else, and they always side with what they see more than what they hear.

_____

_____

_____

_____

_____

_____

_____

_____

_____

_____

Could you lead yourself? What would be the challenge in leading you?

Above, I asked this question in different forms. Think about leading a team, and one of those people is you. Are you capable of leading that person? How would you need to work to influence yourself?

_____

_____

_____

_____

_____

_____

_____

How would you inspire yourself or motivate yourself?

_____

_____

_____

_____

_____

_____

_____

That person knows all your strengths and weaknesses.

How do you overcome them in their eyes?

_____

_____

_____

_____

_____

_____

_____

How well do you serve your people? Do you work

tirelessly to remove obstacles that prevent them from

getting their work done?

_____

_____

_____

_____

_____

_____

_____

What is the difference between a manager and a leader?

Take your daily and weekly tasks, write them all down. Which fall under the definition of management and which fall under the definition of leadership?

_____

_____

_____

_____

_____

_____

_____

_____

_____

_____

_____

_____

_____

_____

_____

_____

_____

If you removed your title, would your people still follow you?

I love, love, love this question. John C. Maxwell introduced me to this question. I can't tell you how many times I have asked it of leaders and witnessed raised eyebrows. There is normally an initial body language that says "of course," but that is followed with a relaxed, almost slumping demeanor when that person actually considers each person they lead and considers if that person would follow them if they did not have the title they had. Are you relying on your title to lead? Do you use authority to lead more than influence? Why?

_____

_____

_____

_____

_____

_____

_____

_____

_____

_____

What can you do to grow your influence? How would you

want a leader to grow their influence with you?

_____

_____

_____

_____

_____

_____

_____

_____

_____

_____

_____

How would that be effective with your people? How do you

know?

_____

_____

_____

_____

_____

_____

It's one thing to lead others. It's another thing to lead

ourselves. Try to ask yourself on a regular basis if you

would follow you. Remember not to ignore the slightest

hesitations. This exercise, if done consistently, could lead to the greatest improvements in your growth as a leader. If you are to ask your people to follow you, you must be willing to do the same. If you are not willing to follow yourself, don't be surprised when you struggle with getting others to do it too.

How Well Do You Communicate?

How our communication is received is more important than our intentions.

You may not want to hear this, but no matter how well intended you are in your communications, how your people perceive your communication is more important than those intentions. Ironically we tend to be blind to the fact that we judge people on how they make us feel, and yet, judge ourselves on our intentions. Do you see the double standard? Think about it: you rarely remember the exact words a leader said, but you easily remember how she made you feel. The dread of having to see her every day, or energized because of the trust she had in giving you the freedom to operate. Do you remember what her intentions were? No you don't. How can you expect others to know what your intentions are? You cannot and you should not. Effective communication requires connection that cultivates trust. Effective communication is the responsibility of the communicator, not the person receiving the communication, especially when the communicator is also the leader.

How well do you connect with those you lead?

I had a colonel in the Marines who knew exactly how to connect with the Marines. Our unit was working feverously to get trucks operational so they could be driven to the port and loaded on ships before our deployment to Kuwait. Our young Marines were working around the clock and on the weekend to get the trucks fixed. Most colonels would have either been at home, or at best, in their office. My colonel put on coveralls and climbed under the trucks with his Marines. He asked them to show him how they did their jobs. He asked them to guide him and teach him how to do what they did. In the process, he asked them about where they were from. How were the conditions in the barracks? How was the food in the chow hall? Years later, when I asked him about it, he told me he learned more in that day than he ever could have from sitting in his office. I learned about him working with the Marines from the Marines themselves. At that time, he was relatively new to being in command of our unit, and I had been detached from the unit for a few months. I was asking the young Marines what their thoughts were about him, and they were quick to share this story. When he communicated from that point forward, his words were iron. There was no confusion in what his intentions were or how the Marines felt about him. This connection made his communication clear and our desire to follow him even clearer.

What do you do to connect with your people? How is that working for you?

One of the most important elements to communicating with those we lead is found in knowing the people we are communicating with. When we take the time to get to know our people, we can better understand the forms of communication that are most effective in getting our intentions across to them.

_____

_____

_____

_____

_____

_____

_____

_____

_____

What do you do to learn about the personal lives, passions, and hobbies of the people you lead?

Do you take the time to allow them to share their ideas with you? Do they trust you? Do they trust that what you are communicating comes from a place within you that has their wellbeing in high consideration? How do you know? I will tell you, from experience, trust plays a critical role in communication. When your people do not trust you, they will assume that your communications have a dual meaning, especially if you have contradicted yourself in the past. One simple example is if you say you value work/life balance, and yet, you work late consistently. What does a leader communicate when he says one thing, but his actions communicate something else? When we conduct ourselves this way as leaders, we are breaking down trust, and that deteriorates how effective we can communicate.

_____

_____

_____

_____

_____

_____

_____

_____

_____

_____

Are you a "Fire and Forget" Communicator? What actions do you take to ensure your intentions come through in your communications?

"Fire and forget" is a military term that originates with shoulder-fired rockets. Some shoulder-fired rockets require the person who fired the rocket to hold in place and guide the rocket on to the target after pulling the trigger. There are other rocket systems, though, that once you pull the trigger, nothing more is required by the person shooting to guide the rocket on to the target, hence, "fire and forget." Far too many leaders communicate this way. They will fire off an email, memo, or announcement without ensuring it hits its mark. I once sat in a client meeting where the leader of the facility was contesting our assessment of how ineffective communication was there. We were reporting to him on an assessment we were hired to conduct. He said to us that if he sends out communications, then he's communicated, and indicated that it was not his responsibility if his people did not understand. I explained to him that just because we have spoken or typed words does not mean we have effectively reached the people. If in our attempts, our people do not respond in the way we intended, we have not been effective, and that responsibility to make corrections falls on us the leader, not on the people whom we are trying to lead.

_____

_____

_____

_____

_____

_____

_____

_____

_____

_____

What can you do as a leader to improve your communication effectiveness?

_____

_____

_____

_____

_____

_____

_____

_____

_____

_____

How can you measure its effectiveness? Think about a

time when you had a leader whom you believe

communicated well. What about his communications

were effective? Why? What steps can you take to improve

your communication? How do you know that would

improve your effectiveness?

_____

_____

_____

_____

_____

_____

_____

_____

_____

_____

_____

How well do you listen?

I once worked with a man who said he could listen while
he was talking. No, I am not joking. He actually claimed
he could listen while he was speaking. It's not possible.
Listening to what your people have to say is critical to
being an effective leader.

Do you know how well you listen? Do you demonstrate
you have listened through follow-up actions? Do you
dismiss ideas your people share with you, only to impose

your own? It's one thing to listen, but it's even better when we can demonstrate to our people that we have listened. Simply remembering a fact that someone has shared with you can demonstrate you care.

_____

_____

_____

_____

_____

_____

_____

_____

_____

_____

_____

_____

Think of a time when you were having a conversation with one of your leaders, how enthused were you to share your story?

_____

_____

_____

_____

_____

_____

How ready were you to share your ideas? Why?

_____

_____

_____

_____

_____

_____

What was your level of enthusiasm when you felt your leaders had interest in your thoughts, ideas, and wellbeing?

_____

_____

_____

_____

_____

_____

_____

How deflated were you when he demonstrated he were not listening? What was the degree of your enthusiasm after learning your leadership had little interest in listening to you?

_____

_____

_____

_____

_____

_____

_____

What do you think the people you lead feel about how well you listen to them? What do you do to demonstrate that you value the thoughts and opinions of your people? Do they know you value their thoughts and opinions? How do they know? Is it important for them to know?

_____

_____

_____

_____

_____

_____

_____

How well do you read body language?

I love conducting meeting in person rather than over the phone. When I do coaching with clients who are not in the same location, I at least try to conduct the sessions over video conference. A great majority of what we interpret in communications comes from what we see more than what we hear. What a person is saying with her facial expressions and body positioning speaks volumes about what she is saying, and how she feels about what you are saying.

We have all seen someone with his arms crossed, leaning back in his seat, slumped. All these indicators tell us that person is not engaged, nor are they buying in to what we are saying.

Do you trust your eyes? What are people communicating to you with their body language?

_____

_____

_____

_____

_____

_____

_____

_____

_____

_____

What does you intuition tell you? Do you ignore it?

_____

_____

_____

_____

_____

_____

Do you ask follow-up or probing questions directed at the body language you are seeing? Or do you ignore body language and rely on words only?

_____

_____

_____

_____

_____

_____

What body language do you project when communicating?
Are you aware of your posture? Have you ever considered
asking those around you what they see in your posture or
body language? What is preventing you from doing so?

_____

_____

_____

_____

_____

_____

_____

_____

_____

_____

Great leaders are great communicators. The difference in effective communication and just plain communicating resides in the connection and the relationship a leader has with her people. We must understand that our intentions may not come through in our communication. We must raise our awareness to this fact so we can take steps to increase our ability to actually communicate what we intend. As leaders, we must be able to read the reactions we receive from our communication and adjust our communication methods on-the-fly.

Exercise:

Ask the people you lead or work with about your communication. If you work in an environment where you may not get honest answers use an anonymous survey (an environment like that should tell you something already). If your people do not feel confident to give you honest, in person feedback, you should already know you have a communication issue. When your people can't come to you with their concerns, you don't have a culture of trust. It's tough to improve when we don't know the truth.

If you desire, capture their responses here: What common themes did you recognize?

_____

_____

_____

_____

_____

_____

_____

_____

_____

Do You Hold People Accountable?

Accountability is critical to credibility.

When people hear the word "accountability," they tend to shy away from it. Far too often, accountability is associated with disciplinary action. Disciplinary action is a last resort to be taken when accountability has failed. Accountability is a cornerstone of leadership. It's where credibility is established for both the one being answered to and the one providing the answers. It is where cultural standards are established and upheld. It requires courage to set, and hold to, a standard of accountability for a leader. Far too many leaders see accountability as a fast track to not being liked by their people, and willfully sacrifice their credibility for likeability. Ironic, don't you think?

What are the lowest standards you permit among your team?

How many people on your team are operating below those standards? If there are people operating below those standards, can you really say your original answer constitutes your lowest standards since you have people on your team operating below that bar?

_____

_____

_____

_____

_____

_____

_____

_____

Now, answer the question again: What is the lowest standard you permit among your team? Is this something you need to address? With whom do you need to address this? Who sets the standards?

_____

_____

_____

_____

_____

_____

_____

_____

Are you willing to have tough conversations with your people?

You don't even have to be a person's leader to hold people accountable. Are you willing to have tough conversations with colleagues or peers who are not living up to the standards of your team, organization, or culture? It takes courage to sit one-on-one with people and speak frankly regarding accountability issues. Are you courageous enough to even hold those whom lead you accountable? No sergeant in the Marine Corps that I know of would ever allow an officer get away with living below Marine Corps standards. It requires a lot of courage to hold peers and leaders accountable.

What does accountability do for your credibility?

_____

_____

_____

_____

_____

_____

_____

What value do you place on your credibility?

_____

_____

_____

_____

_____

If the thought of accountability and tough conversations about organizational standards send a wave of fear over you, ask yourself why?

What are you afraid of?

_____

_____

_____

_____

_____

_____

_____

What are the consequences?

_____

_____

_____

_____

_____

_____

What steps do you think you should take to overcome
your fear?

_____

_____

_____

_____

_____

_____

_____

What are the consequences of not having accountability?

_____

_____

_____

_____

_____

_____

Not just consequences regarding an individual, but what does that say to the entire organization?

_____

_____

_____

_____

_____

_____

_____

Do you think those you lead are blind to when

opportunities for accountability are bypassed? What are

you communicating about yourself as a leader in those

situations?

_____

_____

_____

_____

_____

_____

_____

Have you ever known a successful leader who did not hold

his people accountable? If so, how was he successful?

_____

_____

_____

_____

_____

_____

_____

If you have allowed accountability to slip in the past, how can you re-establish it for the future?

What would work for you, if you had a leader who had never held anyone accountable, and has decided to do so from this point forward?

_____

_____

_____

_____

_____

_____

What could that leader do to establish credibility with you where it was once absent? It's always easy to have started off with accountability and credibility, but the toughest challenge is re-establishing them after they have been lost. Do you have the perseverance to do so?

_____

_____

_____

_____

_____

_____

_____

_____

Are You Willing To Change What You Believe?

"Those who believe they can do something and those who

believe they can't do something are both right."

– Henry Ford

Leadership equals change, and change is a requirement for growth. In order to change, we must be willing to challenge what we believe. Our results are products of our actions and our actions are products of our beliefs. Therefore, we must change our beliefs to change our results. Everything we believe about ourselves is true because in our present state, we are a product of our past beliefs of ourselves. For us to become what we desire to be, we must believe we are already that person.

What do you believe? How has that belief shaped your reality?

What have you always wanted to change about your reality? Have you worked long and hard only to have nothing change?

_____

_____

_____

_____

_____

_____

_____

_____

_____

_____

_____

_____

Work backwards. What would you like your reality to look

like?

_____

_____

_____

_____

_____

_____

_____

For that reality to exist, what would your everyday actions
have to be? And for those actions to happen every day,
what must you believe about yourself? Are you willing to
change what you believe? And, what are the
consequences of changing what you believe? How many
times are you willing to fail?

_____

_____

_____

_____

_____

_____

_____

_____

_____

What would happen if you changed your thoughts?

What are the consequences if you took everything you

believed and turned it upside down in your mind?

_____

_____

_____

_____

_____

_____

_____

What would happen if you changed your beliefs and

thoughts for a day? Is it worth trying? What if the results

were overwhelmingly successful? Could you handle that?

Think about that. Many people unconsciously fear

success because even success brings change to their lives.

If you change your beliefs and your thoughts, they would

change your actions.

_____

_____

_____

_____

_____

_____

_____

_____

_____

_____

If those actions made you wildly successful, what would

that look like? How would you handle it? What would

you have to sacrifice for that success?

_____

_____

_____

_____

_____

_____

_____

_____

_____

_____

_____

How is reality defined for you? What or who shapes your reality?

_____

_____

_____

_____

_____

_____

What are your goals?

Many of us have goals. The problem with goals is that the majority of us don't set them high enough. Why are your goals set to where they are? Are they still attainable?

_____

_____

_____

_____

_____

_____

_____

_____

_____

_____

What would happen if you raised your personal standards?

_____

_____

_____

_____

_____

_____

_____

_____

_____

_____

_____

If you needed 50% more income or even 50% less

expenses to pay for an urgent life event, what changes

would you be willing to make in your thinking and actions

to fulfill that need? What if that way of thinking was your

new standard? We all have our minimum standards.

There are those among us who think that making $50,000

per year is the minimum standard we must attain, and yet

there are others who think $50,000 per month is the

minimum standard, while for others yet, $50,000 per

week is their minimum. This does not just apply to

money. It applies to health, lifestyle, and leadership. A

leader of an organization, team, or group will have the minimum standard they allow. Those leaders who raise their standards will benefit from a team that operates at those standards. What would it require for you to raise your standards?

_____

_____

_____

_____

_____

_____

_____

_____

What would your life look like?

_____

_____

_____

_____

_____

_____

_____

How long does it take to raise your standards?

_____

_____

_____

_____

_____

To what degree do your standards match what you goals are?

_____

_____

_____

_____

_____

_____

Are You Investing In Your Personal and Professional Growth?

We are either growing or withering. Nothing in life remains the same.

Personal and professional growth requires intentional living. We must seek out and act upon avenues that will contribute to our continuous growth. From reading books to enrolling in classes or training programs, from seeking certifications to engaging a coach or mentor, if you are not intentional in engaging in growth activities, you will not grow. The same routine every day, day in and day out, will not change your circumstances. Changing our lives comes at a price. Whether we are sacrificing time, sleep, or finances, there is an investment that is required for growth.

What investment are you making in yourself?

How can you engage in action that will contribute to your personal growth?

_____

_____

_____

_____

_____

_____

_____

What is the return that you seek?

_____

_____

_____

_____

_____

_____

_____

Who controls the level of risk involved in you investing in

yourself? What is the risk?

_____

_____

_____

_____

_____

_____

What is the cause of the risks involved?

_____

_____

_____

_____

_____

What can you do to minimize those risks?

_____

_____

_____

_____

_____

_____

_____

What do you want that investment to achieve?

What does success look like?

_____

_____

_____

_____

_____

_____

_____

_____

What is the feeling you desire? Think of your desires and
goals. Think of a future life when you have achieved those
desires and goals. What is the feeling you have from those
achievements?

_____

_____

_____

_____

_____

_____

_____

_____

_____

How do you feel every morning when you wake up?

_____

_____

_____

_____

_____

_____

_____

What are you willing to sacrifice?

Many people are willing to make sacrifices for their success. What they sacrifice and to what degree is an individual decision. Many sacrifice sleep, family, friends, and health to achieve what they define as success. In that future state of success that you are imagining, what was sacrificed to get there?

_____

_____

_____

_____

_____

_____

Did anyone join you on that journey to success? What did they sacrifice?

_____

_____

_____

_____

_____

_____

_____

_____

_____

_____

_____

If you have things or people you are unwilling to sacrifice, are there ways to achieve your future success without sacrificing them? What other areas or aspects of your life must be sacrificed in order to preserve what you value and achieve success at the same time? Will those sacrifices be tough? Are they worth it?

_____

_____

_____

_____

_____

_____

_____

_____

_____

_____

_____

What is the financial investment you are willing to make in yourself?

Many of us have invested in college degrees, and when you put the amount invested in college in perspective, in many cases, the investment does not outweigh the return. Are you willing to make a financial investment that focusses on a targeted area of your personal and professional growth as a leader? What level of return do you believe you would benefit from in becoming a better leader and person?

_____

_____

_____

_____

_____

_____

_____

We all tend to think of returns on dollars only, but what about time and feelings? What price do you place on those?

_____

_____

_____

_____

_____

_____

_____

What returns would you desire, and in turn, be willing to financially invest in order to achieve? Does your success require a financial investment at all? What is the value you place on your growth?

What Will Your Legacy Be?

"The reason why you can wear that uniform with pride is not because of what you have accomplished. It's because of what the Marines who came before us have accomplished. The pride future Marines have in wearing their uniforms depends on what we do today."
– 1st Lt Chris Waters, USMC

I used to say those words to my platoons as a reminder that a legacy depended on action today to carry to the future, not the actions of the past to carry us to the future. I can proudly say all Marines I served with upheld the legacy handed to them and have handed the torch to future Marines. The Marines serving today wear their uniforms with pride because of the actions of my Marines and countless others from before us.

A legacy is an ultimate testament to a leader. When people who live on after you, think of you and your influence on their lives in their daily actions, you have achieved a level of leadership that is immortal. Look at Martin Luther King Jr., George Washington, and Mother Teresa. Today, people look to their lives and their words for guidance. If they were alive today, and we had an opportunity to sit with them and ask them anything, we would all jump at the opportunity. The level of leadership and influence they achieved in their lives will live on. That's the true legacy of a leader's life well lived.

So, I leave you with this one final question: What will your legacy be?

When your day to leave this world arrives, how will you have impacted the lives of others? Will there be people who look to your guidance, even in your absence, because of the influence you had in their lives? Will there be people who remember the words you spoke, or the actions you took? Will they ask: "What would they have done if they were here in this situation?" You can't control the decisions people make in your absence, but you can influence them. What will your final chapter be? What will people say about your life and how you influenced them? Don't answer based on your current state. Answer based on what you will achieve.

Conclusion

It is not my intention for this book to lead you to believe that this is the full essence of coaching. The beauty and magic of coaching resides in the relationship between the coach and the coaching participant or client. A good coach recognizes body language, fluctuations in language and tone, hesitations and enthusiasms. A good coach does not have the questions planned, but rather is so present in the moment that the questions present themselves as the sessions and the relationship progresses. It is my intention, however, to introduce to you the possibilities that coaching could unlock for you and your potential. It is my desire for this book to start to thaw the ice that binds you and your success. It is my hope and desire that you use this as a catalyst that helps you turn up the heat even more in your journey to realizing your potential as a leader and as a person. As my mentor has told me, I will pass to you. Our potential has no limits. The limits we have in our lives are created by ourselves. We have the power to define those limits as well as eliminate them all together. Which will you choose to do? I wish you success on your journey!

About The Author

Christopher D. Waters is a leadership coach, author, speaker, and consultant. From his service in the United States Marines to the corporate world, he has dedicated the past sixteen years to developing the leaders around him. In 2012 he founded Agoge Leadership Development LLC in order to live his passion to develop and coach entrepreneurs, professionals, and organizations in realizing their leadership potential. He has also spoken to student athletes at the college and high school levels on the subjects of teamwork and embracing failure as a stepping stone to success. Chris lives with a dedication to serve America in order to improve, secure, and protect its future. Chris believes in the vision of a society that is populated by moral leaders who place their values at the forefront of every decision they make and action they take. It's leaders like those who will make the future a safer and more fulfilling place for our children.

www.ingramcontent.com/pod-product-compliance
Lightning Source LLC
Chambersburg PA
CBHW020916180526
45163CB00007B/2762